From Hotmess Express to Achievable Goals

You Have to Know Where You Came From To Know Where You Are Going

Keneshia Renee

From Hotmess Express to Achievable Goals

You Have to Know Where You Came From To Know Where You Are Going

From Hotmess Express to Achievable Goals

Copyright © 2020 by Keneshia Renee Raymond

All Rights Reserved

ISBN: 9798672219806

Imprint: Independently published

Printed August 2020

All Photo's: Regina Kay Photography

Cover Design: Diamond Raymond

For

My mama, my sisters, my dad, and my auntie. Thank you for believing in me and teaching me to believe in myself. You are my light when mine is dim. Thank you for always shining! Thank you to my angels in heaven.

Foreword

Good for you! You have just taken a big step towards getting on track and moving forward in your personal and professional life. Take a moment to celebrate! Each small step makes a difference; one foot in front of the other is how amazing, transformative, innovation gets done.

I know this book will be a part of your success story because I know Keneshia Raymond. In fact, it was Keneshia's expertise with goal setting that brought her into my life. I have had the pleasure of working with Keneshia at our nonprofit, Startup Tucson. When we were hiring for Keneshia's position the CEO and I had a seemingly impossible wish-list in mind; this dream person needed to be a stone-cold expert in business strategy (ideally with some experience raising VC capital and maybe even a little IPO experience under their belt), they needed to be over-the-top passionate about helping entrepreneurs succeed, they needed to be committed to making entrepreneurship equitable and accessible to all, and on top of it all, they needed to be both a brilliant teacher and mentor. Like I said, an impossible dream person. But then, enter the one and only Keneshia Raymond.

As part of the interview process, we asked each candidate to prepare a short mock-class on a topic they were passionate about. Keneshia, our very first interviewee, steps up and gives a five-minute presentation on goal setting that had my CEO and I scrambling to take notes to get it all down as fast as she could teach it, completely knocking our socks off.

When the interview was over, I turned to my CEO "So...we just canceled all the other interviews, right?" We had struck gold!

And now you have too.

Enjoy this book and let the process transform your work as Keneshia has done for us.

Warmly,
Dre Thompson, Executive VP Startup Tucson

Contents

Chapter Six - Let's plan & celebrate

Introduction

Hey! And welcome if we have not met. I am Keneshia, the lady behind this book. For the last eleven years, in addition to being an entrepreneur, I have worked with entrepreneurs and coached them on some of the exact things, found right here in this book.

Funny story, this book has been perching on my vision board for some time now and fear had me on pause by feeling like the task might be a bit too daunting, but I challenged myself on Facebook live to write a book in 30 days and y'all I did it!

So here we go..When I decided I wanted to write a book a couple of years ago, I knew I wanted to write something fun that could empower and connect me to people. It was a few years ago and at the time I was heavily consumed in the wedding industry.

I decided I wanted to write all about creating and designing a beautiful wedding space for wedding planners. I sat down and started to write, without so much as an outline or anything to that effect, and just started penning down my thoughts. Well, life got busy and it was one of those out of sight, out of mind instances, but I'm going to get to it...one day.

Well, I am finally sitting here, writing this book, and the "old" book is still sitting in a draft folder with about maybe a total of ten pages in rough draft. So when I reached the definite conclusion that I was really going to write a book, I knew I needed to write about something that really fired me up, motivated me, and something that really excites and scares me simultaneously. All this, while cultivating the process I created for myself and my business. Over the last ten years, I have been building a business that I love - working with entrepreneurs and educating them on all the things I have learned. Which was a culmination of the good, the bad and the ugly. while running their own businesses so that they don't have to make the same mistakes I have made in my company's infancy phases.

I provide guidance to them on how, using a proven strategy can take their business to the next level, and how using this strategy that I developed can give them a solid foundation to launch, grow or expand their respective businesses.

I have always had big, audacious dreams and goals, but I didn't always know how to achieve them, which is one of the hardest things for me to admit. To be completely honest and to give you a little background about myself which I seldom share, because being vulnerable is just not my thing.

Growing up, maybe around the elementary school phase, my biggest goal was to live to see 18. See, I grew up in the hood of LA. I have seen many not live to the age of 18. So yes, I dreamed that one day, I would run away and go to college in New York., But first I had to live to actually see that day.

We moved away from the LA area, to La Mirada when I was twelve. As soon as we moved away, I was able to open my eyes to all the opportunities around me. My mind opened up to the possibility of even dreaming towards something bigger.

Even though my mom always told me, "You can be whatever you want to be, and you can accomplish, whatever you set out to accomplish.". As I sit here now, we are mourning the loss of a beautiful soul gone too soon. She had some big goals for her own life as well as for the lives of her children, and I am asking myself; What would have been different if I had done this sooner?

To give you a bit of insight, for a very long time I struggled with The Impostor Syndrome. I didn't feel like I was smart enough to be the VP of a company, or that I would never achieve it, so WHY even bother trying. Naturally, right now, as we speak I have the tendency to not write down my dreams and to transfer them into goals, which is one of the main reasons that it may take me longer to achieve them.

After doing research and listening to what seemed like a million podcasts and watching so many webinars , I realised that I was not alone. There were so many people struggling with one; how to set a real goal , and two; how to accomplish them.

A couple of years ago I made a conscious decision to start taking some of that advice that I heard to heart and to start to really put them into action, but to make them more applicable and relevant to myself and make it work for me. See, there are a ton of people teaching others the basics in the art of Goal Setting, and not everyone's methods might work for you specifically, you have to take what you learn and take ownership of it and make it your own.

When you think about all the things you want to accomplish in life, you also have to think about who you will be once you've accomplished those goals. Once I started to think about what I wanted from life and who I wanted to be, that's when I was able to start chipping away at these big goals that I wanted to accomplish and started breaking them into more achievable pieces.

I recall my stint in corporate America, and all I wanted to do was progress in the company I was working for. I was making the moves and doing all the right things, but my boss at the time was not trying to hear me, was not actually acknowledging the work I was doing, or even trying to see me for who I was.

He promoted people around me and I just kind of bided my time to keep a job. The 2008 recession hit, we were put on furlough and then later laid off. As we were preparing for the last week, we had a ton of staff meetings and in the last one, in front of a room full of people, he said to me " I am so surprised that you lasted this long, we had been trying to find a way to let you go for a while now, your work was great, but you didn't connect and become friends with other people on the team."

To me that was a trigger. I was young, in my twenties and hot headed, so that really stuck with me. I knew at that moment; one, I would never go back to corporate America, and if I did I would find a job that was going to pay me to be more people centric, and two; never be treated like crap by a boss just to get a paycheck and having to endure never-ending narcissism.

In 2009 /2010 when we were laid off, I knew at that moment I would never strive to build someone else's dream again, but I had no Idea what that really meant for me in particular . In 2010 I became what I refer to as an "accidental entrepreneur" and started a cupcake business that rocked y'all and that was my departure point on my very first journey in trying to figure out how to conquer my goals in the business sense.

Fast forward to now. It's 2020 and I had some big goals planned for this year, and with the current crisis it has been slow-going. But you know what? I am not stopping! I will continue to keep chipping away, one piece at a time, until I reach my goals.

Lessons I have learned over the years have taught me that it is beautiful to dream, but to actually make these dreams a reality, I would need to figure out how to turn the dream into a goal and make those goals materialize.

So this is not going to be just another dream for me, this book was a goal and together we are making it happen, and my biggest wish is for you to experience the same. I want you to dream big! I want you to be the best you that you can be! I want you to make today and the next day the best day. As you are jumping into this book we are going to be doing the work in a collaborative effort. We are going to talk about your big goals and we are going to work through your goals to turn them from dreams into reality.

Whilst, doing my research and thinking about writing this book, I realized there are so many journals out there for you to buy and just write down all your goals, and that's great! I too have a ton actually and I am currently writing in three of them to be precise.

What I found to be lacking, or there were very few of, were the books to tell you how to really get started, jump in, and walk you through how to actually create goals that are attainable. Goals that you can actually reach out and touch. So, friend we are going to do just that, I am not here to be your cheerleader (FYI, I was an actual Cheer Coach at one point in my life, so I can give you a great cheer with pom-poms and the whole dog and pony show) I am here to give you the tools, and knowledge you need to help you reach your goals.

Most times people wait until the end of the year, or the beginning of the new year to set their goals, or even better, they say: "I will do this on Sunday or Monday when the new week starts. I am saying throw that negativity out the door and close it!

There is no better time to start setting new goals, growing your business, or changing yourself in your life than this time, as in , right now. This is the time to change yourself, grow yourself and make a change that will not just take you into Sunday, but that will take you into next year.

Stop waiting to achieve that goal that has been in your mind for the last couple of years, stop procrastinating and just get it done. Your goals were not made to sit on a shelf, your goals were made to be conquered and to be achieved!

As you are reading this, remember you have already accomplished your first goal, you showed up for yourself and you are taking the steps to make your life, your business and your future brighter. There is nothing like accomplishing a goal that makes your heart sing.

So grab a notepad, grab your favorite beverage, wine, coffee, tea, beer. As for me I am having a Margarita, with a dash of lime and a salty rim - and let's get this done.

Chapter One

Crafting Your Foundation

The Mission Statement

T he Mission Statement is a formal statement that you, your clients , and/or staff can buy into. It should describe the people you want to target, the products and services that you offer, as well as what makes it unique. The mission statement is the power statement, and represents what you and your business stand for. As we get into this chapter we will do a deeper dive and really flesh out the statement.

In order for us to move forward and create solid goals, you need to create a mission statement. Now this is tailored to you, your life and your goals. If you are creating life goals for your mission statement they should be completely tailored to your life's mission, and if you are setting goals for your business you need to write a mission statement that is tailored to your business.

So how do I write a mission statement?

Well, your mission statement starts with your WHY.
- WHY is this so important to you?
- What is it that you hope to accomplish and,
- WHY do you want to accomplish it?

The WHY in your life or in your business forms the foundation of what will continue to propel you forward in achieving your goals.

Everything starts with your WHY

In order for you to create your mission statement we need to figure out the WHY behind what you're doing. One of the most frequently asked questions I get is; WHY is the WHY important and how do I define my WHY. Your WHY" is pivotal because it is the departure point of the actual object you are in the process of creating and it is the reason behind everything you do.

Everything we do in life is mentally or otherwise known as psychologically done on purpose and with intent. To put this into simpler terms, think about when you get up in the morning, what do you do first? Do you turn off your alarm and head to the shower? If so, WHY?
Because it has become routine and this is how your body reacts to the alarm going off ? Or is it because you made a subconscious decision that this is what your morning routine is going to look like.

At some point in your life, you made a decision that this is your morning routine and this is what you are going to continue to do everyday, correct? So WHY?

WHY is this the morning routine you picked for yourself? WHY is this what gets you going in the morning? Now what would be different if you change your routine?

Take this same example and apply it to your daily life, but in all other areas and not just your morning routine. Ask yourself questions like;

- WHY do I want to accomplish the things that I want to accomplish?
- How will it actually look like when I accomplish just this one goal?
- How will it make me feel to accomplish this one

goal?
- What will the impact be in my life if I accomplish this one goal?

As you are answering these questions for yourself for every answer, I want you to ask yourself WHY? Picture this exercise like a five year old child continuing to ask you WHY:

"Mom I want to go outside" and you respond to say "Not right now son"

"But WHY mom?"
"Because it's cold".
WHY is it cold Mom"?
"Because it's raining."
"But mom WHY is it raining"?

You get the idea, you need to be the nag in your own head that continues to ask yourself WHY. When you get down to the root of the WHY, that is when your emotions will kick in and you will be completely pissed at yourself or me, lol! And then you will have the true definition of the actual WHY behind what you are creating.

When I set out to write this book for the third time, I completely started from scratch. I decided that I was going to use the exact same system that I teach to others, as well as use in my own businesses.

Sitting down with a notepad and a pen, I asked myself WHY it was important for me to write this book and what makes me qualified to teach y'all how to set goals. Yes, I do teach this at many of my workshops and I also teach it to my clients.

Speaking at public events and coaching one on one, versus creating a book, is very different, so in my head I'm thinking who the hell told me I can write a book. I was a complete naysayer in my head, but then I decided to call my own bluff and get it out.

Remember when I told you in the beginning of this chapter to grab a piece of paper? Well now's the time to get to work. Write down your WHY. Write everything that is at the top of your mind, don't overthink, just dump it out on paper.

There are no right or wrong answers. This is your WHY, so tell your mind to take a knee, because this is your time to let your mind be free and write down every honest thought that you have had about the WHY behind the goals that you are going to accomplish.

Set an alarm for 5 minutes. I want you to write about all of your WHY.

Remember, your WHY is personal and unique to YOU. It can be as big as growing your business to a six figure business, to wanting to make an extra 1k this month. It can be a family goal to take a vacation to Disneyland, or just make it through the summer with no major meltdowns.

These are your WHY's and no one is here to judge you and you my friend can not judge yourself. In life, we have to teach ourselves to be both honest, but kind to ourselves at the same time. We are our own biggest critics and now is not the time for you to criticize yourself. Right now you are Beyonce, and you woke up like this, and you can do no wrong!

Here are some sample questions to ask yourself when identifying your WHY;

What is my WHY?

WHY is this important?

How will your life change with this WHY?

What makes your WHY special?

Your **mission statement** is derived from your WHY, and the mission statement is the large version of your purpose sentence. It should tell a story of WHY you do exactly what you do and who you do it for. Your purpose statement is the intent behind what you are doing and how you intend to do this.

Think of your **mission statement** as the purpose statement that catapults your business to where you want it to be. It is what you check in with when you are making big plans for what comes next in your business.

I think of it as my calorie checker when I'm trying to get summer body ready, do I need this Margarita? Did I count it into my calorie tracker? Ok, now I can have it! Lol, let's be real, I am having that Margarita but I do check in with myself and my purpose statement.

For your business you can't check and do it anyway, you need to make sure it is mission aligned and it is telling the story you want to continue to tell in your business to propel your business forward. When it comes to business, you have to be your own Accountability Partner.

Vision Statement

The Vision Statement is where you can be selfish. It is a big goal for your company or your life. This is where you get to dream a bit before you put the dream into action and make it a goal.

Now your **vision statement** is the bigger picture, this is exactly what you see for your business or life in the future. This is the big plan, the one that when you look at your business in five to ten years you see, you can touch it and you can feel it.

This is where you have all the space to create a vision that you will break down into goals to make it a reality. So dream a bit, let your mind be free to dream of the big audacious goal. Create the vision that you want for your life or business, completely limitless! There's no limit!.

Core Values

In order to achieve your goals we have to create the **core values** of your life or business. This is not something you really have to dig deep to find, you already know this. This is something that you probably already live by, your daily Coat of Arms in your arsenal.

Your core values are very heart-centered. These values should be something that you and your team live by and also the values that are at the heart in your client-facing relations and rapports.

It is very important for the people that you connect with

to know what values you live by, as well as the values that your company embodies, so they know what to expect up front and it's never a surprise. My thoughts are that you always want to set both yourself and your clients up for success. When they know what to expect in the beginning they are more eager to work with you in the future.

Now take some time and create your WHY, the mission statement, vision statement, and core values. These are the hierarchy of creating meaningful goals in your life or your business. Remember that this is not homework, this is your life and in order to create the goals you actually want, you have to do the work, not just read the book . FYI, I do love that you are reading the book and well done on getting this far.

So get to writing.

Chapter Two

You have to know where you came from to know where you are going

If you never reflect on where you have been, how do you know where you are going?

Some years into my wedding planning career I took a Designer job for a conference and I was stoked. It was not only huge for my career doing my first big conference event in the Bay area for the wedding industry, but amazing for the space I was in. It was a pioneer in the field of wedding technology conferencing. When the job was over I knew I wanted more but wasn't entirely sure what exactly that was.

At the end of that year I sat back and reflected on what went right and how I could grow more, and WHY I wanted to grow. The next year they hired me as the VP of the company and I was floored.

I remember thinking OMG they had to have made a mistake, but also thinking I worked my butt off to get here and I was so excited and I deserved this - I deserved this moment!

The year I was hired as VP, we decided to take this conference on tour and did a local conference. It was crazy as hell! That year I provided the Opening Address at the conference, in addition to designing the conference, and managed to invite an amazing Keynote Speaker among all the other great speakers to Hawaii.

I wanted this conference to be one for the books, and it

was. I remember sitting on the plane to Hawaii in tears, I was so happy and so proud of what I had accomplished, but still there was so much doubt in my heart, creating much inner conflict.

Now, I know that I am a kickass Event Planner but there was something so not right about this whole thing. We had an amazing two day conference with an opening party at a celebrity bar, called Fleetwoods on Front Street, right off the water, at sunset an hour after the rain cleared, and so many people enjoyed themselves.

As for me, I sat on the beach for 7 days and enjoyed every inch of the warm, white sand beneath my toes.. This conference was one that my industry yearned for and one that they absolutely loved. It was a space for the tech industry that was creating tools for wedding professionals to meet wedding professionals, and learn about their needs before they created them, so a WeddingTech event if you will.

It was also the first time an event of this magnitude was hosted in Hawaii for the wedding industry. It brought people from all over the island including some of the big tech heads from the big Island. It was an absolute success for our company as well as the wedding industry.

I was so honored to have our traditional opening blessing by our friend Branscomb's wife, and our opening Keynote Mrs. Rachel Hollis, graced the stage. This all happened before her best selling book *Girl Stop Apologizing* was released, but it was the perfect time to have her grace our stage.
She shared her experiences with our industry professionals about her life as a wedding planner and transitioning into becoming a lifestyle blogger, growing her company and now having mogul status. That conference was

phenomenal! We even gave away a wedding via Skype to a pretty cool couple, who I am still friends with today.

What I realized after the event, was that even though I had this amazing position, and we were making history in the wedding industry, it was out of sync with my WHY, and it did not align with my core values, but I was in it and i'm not a quitter so I stayed and built a company that soon closed shop.

As much as I loved what I was doing, my heart told me the truth and I didn't listen. This my friends is WHY it's important to reflect on the picture in its entirety. It means not just reflecting on the happy, but also on the crappy. It's also a time when I say listen to your heart. The combination of both your mind and your heart will give you clues when something is not right.

It is very important to reflect on what the last six months and the last year looked like for you. Through your reflection you will start to see a pattern of which goals you achieved and the goals you didn't achieve, and WHY.

There's that WHY word again, it will continue to be a common theme throughout this process, so get comfortable with getting to know the WHY and attain a solid understanding of the pivotal importance of its role in your life and your goals.

The aim of this practice is not to make you feel bad for not achieving your goals. This is a time for gaining an understanding as to WHY you didn't achieve your goals and if you did achieve them, what you did differently that made them come alive.

WHY did you achieve this goal and not achieve the other

goal? If you have written down goals in the past, grab that notebook and bring it to help you review and peruse over what you have written down.

So let's jump into reviewing your past goals. Write down the goals you set for the last six months or the last year. Don't skip the little ones, just write them all out. Once you have them all written out , want you to put a star or highlight the ones you actually accomplished, and then write a note of WHY", or how you accomplished them, and lastly, WHY they were important to you.

Use the same procedure with the goals you have not achieved and write down if they were truly important and WHY you believe you didn't achieve them.

I am a very visual person so normally what I do is create a vision board of my goals for the year, which for me means tons of post-it-notes. As I accomplish them I take them down, so I feel a sense of accomplishment I also keep a list of my goals to accomplish for the year so I have them both in a digital version and an actual visual representation for me to look at everyday. So, as I jump into reviewing, I use my list and put the post it notes back up, giving them two categories: the goals I achieved and the ones that got away.

The reason we are getting into detail with the "what " and the WHY, is so we can see at what point you did not reach your goal and how you can make some changes going forward to help you reach your goals.

We also want to identify what goals you succeeded at accomplishing and what you did to accomplish them. So as you are moving forward we are taking the good habits with us and leaving the bad habits behind.

Now that we have done the reviewing it's time to reflect on what you accomplished last year. Write down the top goals you accomplished or move your sticky notes around and figure out WHY they were important.

What made them more special than the other goals you accomplished? Reflect on how happy you were when you reached that specific goal and what did you do when you reached that goal.

Now celebrate yourself because you did that, you achieved your goals!

Transport your mind and body back to that exact moment of the joy you felt when you reached that goal, and remain in that cocoon of happiness for a while, taking it in.

Now, go back to the goals you did not accomplish and think about what would have been different if you actually accomplished those goals and then live in that exact moment for a brief period of time. Live in, and picture yourself how it would have felt like if you had accomplished them.

The exact feeling you felt when accomplishing the big goal is the exact feeling you should have when you are writing your goals. See, your goals are your dreams, those big moments you want to have in your life, but when we don't have those big moments, we get down on ourselves by comparing our beginnings to other peoples' ends.

We also sometimes get a bit of Impostor Syndrome, because we don't feel like we can do what we say we can do. That's all crap my friend! You can accomplish anything you put your mind to. You just have to have a plan to get it done and work and rework that plan till you reach success. It's a constant, living work in progress, that evolves as time passes by.

Creating a plan is the first step to achieving your goals

Some of you might find that you may be a lot like I once was. You have all the goals, but never wrote them down on paper. This hints at the fact that you may never achieve them because you never made them real, and because you never wrote them down, you never shared them with anyone and there was no one to hold you accountable.

Does that sound familiar? Are you nodding your head with me now? I too have been there before, but I quickly learned if I want to get it done and actually accomplish a goal that I could be proud of, I had to do the work and put in the required effort.

As you are going through this book and really breaking down your top goals I want you to ask yourself WHY.

WHY is it important to me? How will it change my life and how will it make me feel like when I accomplish this goal?

Keep a separate notebook and pen, write this down, so when you feel yourself slipping or you are doubting yourself you will remember your WHY. Now's the time to change our habits and create new habits by writing down our goals, creating an action plan and conquering them like a boss.

Your WHY is at the core of everything you do and will be the main reason you continue to push forward. So ask yourself, is my WHY big enough?

Chapter Three

Why They Fail

WHY your goals fail

There have been so many times I have set out to have this phenomenal year and to accomplish these audacious goals, but then fail short at actually getting them accomplished. I remember a few years ago I set out to scale my wedding experience from not just local but having regional presence as well.

Ideally, I wanted to hit 10 states in a year, all while running my actual wedding planning business, my educational business and still being the VP of the company I worked for. Needless to say, I hit the ground running and started at home.

At that time I lived in the Bay Area and let me tell you the first wedding experience was packed, between myself and the venue we had an amazing encounter. It was like nothing they had seen in the Bay Area before. It was an entire experience, a journey of sorts , not just another wedding show.

The couples had a chance to visualize how their wedding look and felt like through the eyes of this show. Y'all I even had Fire Dancers! It was phenomenal! As a result of the raging success I resolved to take this show on the road.

I proceeded to start booking these 10 venues with another planner who joined and we sat out to take on the industry and disrupt it in a good way, all the while giving brides a chance to really experience a wedding without being sold services they might not want or need but actually buying into what they ideally desired.

That year we worked so hard, even though we only had 3 shows and they ended up being all local, and we had about 50% capacity booked. Did we have a great time? Yes we did! Did our guests enjoy it? Yes they did!

Our vendors were amazing and it boosted their respective businesses in turn. We also helped with their marketing and helped them grow their businesses. What we didn't do is actually reach our own goals.

We didn't meet our actual expectations and here's WHY.

In order for us to actually conquer our goals, we have to know WHY our goals actually fail. Remember , I said *you have to know where you came from to know where you are going.*

The Number One Reason Our Goals Fail Is Because:

1.   We confuse dreams / aspirations with actual goals

We all have a dream to wake up early, work out everyday, spend more time with the family and maybe even one day start a six figure business. Dreams are great and I encourage you to take some time to put your head in the clouds and dream. Dream freely, dream big and dream often! Dreaming about all the things you want to do and launch is wonderful.

Dreaming about waking up early and working out is also a great thing (I was out when the phrase getting up early came in, lol), but in order to turn that big dream into reality we have to make it a goal. Your dream has to be turned into this tangible, realistic thing that is not a maybe , or one day I will have that, or maybe next year I will get that. For example, it has to be on April 15,2021 - I will achieve that thing! You need to be that specific!

A dream is a goal with no action. It's kind of like a party without cake. A party is not a party if there is no cake, Without a delectable slice of cake, it's just a gathering of people! A goal is a dream with an actionable, tangible plan.

It's something you can touch, measure, and actually achieve, providing you have an action plan and you are actively working on the plan. We can continue to dream, but the dream is now followed by an action plan and a dream with a plan is a goal!

I am going to give it to you one more time in my best 90's rap voice for the people in the back with the cheap seats: "A dream + Plan = goal"!

I need you to hear me when I say dreaming is the beginning step to the magic you will create. But if you leave it in your head, just sitting idle, this big dream you have, it will never surmount to anything. Take that dream, write it down, get it out of your head and create a plan so that you achieve the goal!

2. *The goal is too big*

I know what you are saying, she just told me to dream big, reach for the stars and make it happen. Yes, that is exactly what I said! I want you to dream and reach for the stars but your goal should never be so overwhelming, that it derails your ability to achieve it.

We can achieve our goals but as we head on to our approach, we have to break it down into chunks. Think of your goal setting like making a PB&J sandwich, what is the first thing you do before you even have the bread in your hand? There are steps and processes to everything we do. Just take your time and breathe through.

When you set big, lofty goals with no plan, and jump in front of a moving train, you better believe you are setting yourself up for failure! Setting goals that are too big and not specific and detailed enough, will only leave you with heartbreak, despair and feeling indifferent.

Subsequently, it will take you even longer to want to get back out there and try again.

3.   *We think our goals need to be demanding & hard*

I am not entirely sure when or how we as humans started to think this way, but I have heard it over and over again. People saying "If my goal is not demanding, and my goal is not hard enough - it's just no good.

I am here to bust that myth, stat! Who has the actual right to tell you how hard your goal has to be and what they are supposed to be? Nobody! Your goal can be as easy or as hard as you want it to be.

There are no metrics that say your goal bears no significance, because it's not hard or demanding. Therefore, please as you are setting your goals, take time to set the goals that mean something to you, whether it be in your personal life or your business.

These goals are for you, and for no one else but yourself. Remember, that your goals always check in with your WHY and your WHY checks with your mission, vision and your core values.

When you set these large, imposing goals that are too hard to achieve, and then you get stuck, because it causes you to have Analysis Paralysis. Ergo, we have to take a step back and figure that out as well.

Your goals are not for you to overthink and over-analyse. What you need to do is find out WHY they are a goal and WHY they are important.

4.   *We don't have proper systems in place*

Yes, many of us have wonderful notepads that we write everything in, (the notepad of broken dreams), while others decide to keep everything in their head and it goes nowhere. When I start the journey with a new client, I ask them what the goals are that they hope to accomplish, and how they are currently tracking those goals.

Most times they are in their head, written on a notebook they have to go find, or on a Trello or Asana board where they put them in orphan or White Elephant state, never to go back and revisit them. Then as we are going through the process, they say "I do have a system.

But do you really have one if you have to go look for it? I think of these proverbial "systems" as the trunk in the basement that you know is there, you know you put some good stuff in there, but you never go back to check it out.

The foundation to actually achieve your goals is for you to

have a proper approach in place to change the dream into a goal, and the goal into reality.

You're probably thinking - this lady is crazy! But I promise you I'm not! We as humans run on routine and create routines and form habits for our lives. We will now be taking that same thought process and creating a routine or a system to work for you when creating your goals.

If you don't create a system, you will continue to feel like you are on a stationary bike going nowhere. You will continue to make promises to yourself, that you will probably not keep. Cue the end of the year post where you post about all the stuff you didn't get accomplished but next year is going to be a better year and you will even attempt to revisit the dashed dreams and goals!.

No! Now is going to be a better year. Tomorrow is going to be a better day. Creating a system is what will set you up for success over and over every time.

Where I failed in creating this wedding experience in 10 states are all the things just listed above. The goals were too big, and I felt in order for it to succeed, we had to successfully host the event in all 10 states, in year one. This could have been amazing if I managed to start small and then scaled in the following years. If I had taken the time to put together a proper system, and worked a plan, we would have seen great results. Looking at it retrospectively now I can tell you everything we did wrong, but I can also tell you everything that went right, and I celebrate it all! Knowing where I came from and when moving forward, I continue to reflect on this moment to help me keep the momentum..

Goal setting is not rocket science, but it can feel like it is when you have to sit down and actually try to figure out how to do it. It's one of those things that everyone wants to cheer about at the end of every year, including me, but no one wants to get down in the weeds with you to get it done and trust me, I know how frustrating that can be.

A few years ago when I really started taking my goal setting seriously, I hit Pinterest and I hit it hard! Looking for anything I could find on goal setting. I read so many blogs and articles and still had no actionable plans on how to start with the goal setting process.

Therefore, I took a little bit from all the blogs, and started creating my goals. In came the sticky notes and up it went on my wall! A visual representation appeals to me, so for me the only way to get them on paper were by way of post-it notes. It was also so simple to move around, that I actually enjoyed it immensely!

Side note: If you have a white board (I recently found these post-it clingy's that work just like post it's) I also use giant post-it's to create my board, to then add more post-it's to or write directly on them.

My goal and biggest hearts' desire for you, is to enjoy setting your goals and making all the right moves to create a plan and succeed.

Chapter Four

Systems That Work For You Not Against You

Your system should be like the recipe for a perfect Margarita

Alright, now let's take a journey to create the proper process that is going to work for you. See, goals' setting is not rocket science, it's like a perfect Margarita. It involves a lot of passion, followed by some consistency, topped with action and rimmed with a whole lot of hustle.

It took me a very long time to develop and perfect a system that worked for me. I have failed a lot as an entrepreneur, which in turn means I have learned a lot - the hard way!

Starting out I was the person that wanted to do everything myself. I didn't want to listen to anyone, and only wanted to use what I thought was going to work for me. My mom always said a hard head makes a soft behind, and yes that is so true! For me that was having big dreams with no plan, which equates to disappointment and no actual results.

Big dreams with no results also equals comparing yourself to the next person, which FYI is never the right thing to do. We are all different and unique! Enter the Impostor Syndrome (H-E-L-L-O!). If you are not familiar with Impostor Syndrome, it's when you suffer from feelings of inadequacy and self-doubt.

You may be thinking "I am not smart enough, or good enough to do what I had dreamt up in my mind". I had all those feelings and more, but they are just feelings. They get into your head and set you back, and then you continue to question everything you do. We need to brush them off and carry on!

The feelings of Imposter Syndrome held me back. It also should have been the last thing I was feeling because I knew what I was doing and I was a subject matter expert. It was the fact that I had no system , and I was flying by the seat of my pants literally that had me in a moment and feeling like this. So I never got started, which in turn meant I never achieved any of my goals.

My whole goal for this book is to educate you on a system that you can use in your life and in your business, in the hopes to help you avoid the same mistakes I made. Yes, I learned from them and I have grown as a result of the lessons learnt, but I would have rather preferred to have had some guidance, and maybe even have taken some notes from all of the classes I took in the beginning.

So let's talk about a proper goal setting process. A proper system is not downloading the next big app. A proper system is something you want to go back to and revisit and constantly reshape and rework, like a rough diamond.

It is easy to update, and something that is highly visible. A key component of a good system is that it should be something that you can look at, and understand where you want to be in the following year.

A proper system is retro in nature, with plain old markers, paper and some colorful post-it notes. The only way to really see your goals is to get them on paper, so I want you to grab some paper, post-it notes, markers or your favorite pen and let's get cracking.

In chapter one we talked about creating a mission, vision and core values statement. These are the three pillars for your foundation for all the goals you are going to create. These are your checkpoints and anytime you create a goal you need to check in with your mission statement to determine if it aligns.

Is it going to move your vision forward and does it truly value the core values of your company in mind, and then does it answer your core mission which is your WHY?

It might come across as overwhelming and you don't have to do that in the beginning, but you do need to check in to make sure you are working towards your plan. I want you to create a pyramid, it is the hierarchy of your goals and as you work your goals this will come into play (see diagram below).

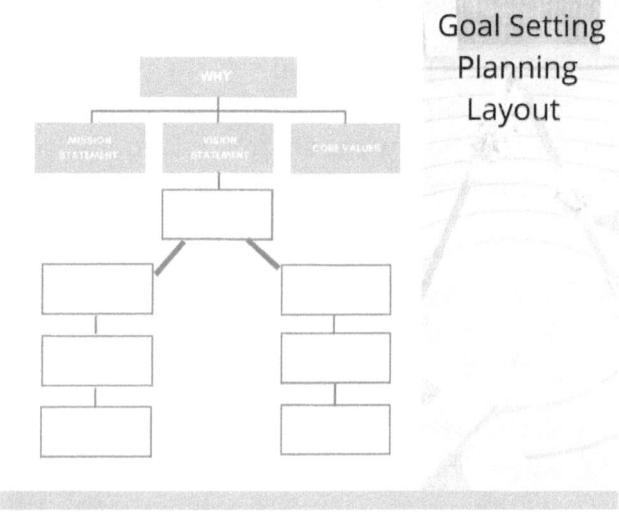

Goal Setting
Planning
Layout

Start by writing all your goals on your paper and transfer them on to a post-it note. For each goal you want to add them to a separate post-it note, or if you are using paper you can write two on a page so you can tear it and add your WHY or more content.

Take about 10 minutes of uninterrupted time and write down all the goals you want to accomplish this year, in your business or in your personal life. Remember it is never too late to make a change and start setting goals, we don't have to wait till the inception of January each year to start afresh!

As an entrepreneur, I am fully aware that we can get stuck in statements such as "I will start this on Sunday or next quarter". We get so caught up and consumed in this trap, that we forget that it's ok to start now.

I know this is also where the procrastination takes over. We have to embrace our business or our personal life where it is at right now, and be real with ourselves about it. So, if you are reading this on a Wednesday, go ahead and set the goals, because every single day starts anew and who said the beginning of the year is the only fresh start you get? *Yo, you woke up this morning, so let's get it!*

Now that you have taken the time to really jump in, and do a brain dump, I want you to make columns. You can name your columns whatever you want but they should be along the lines of the most important, kind of important, two year project, fun to do, and going to make me actual revenue.

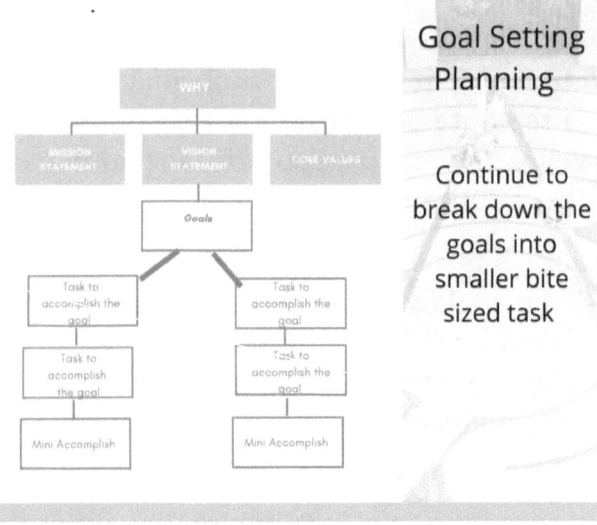

You can now start moving your goals around and adding them into the columns, if anything fits into two buckets/columns make a second post-it and add it in both. Anything that is a big win for your business should not only be important, but revenue generating in some kind of way.

This could be a set up for revenue or a CTA (call to action), that will turn into revenue. Growth is all part of the system to get you to profit and capital growth.

Once you have all of your goals into separate buckets, and you know exactly what is important and where it fits in your business, it's time to now break down the WHY for each of the goals.

Firstly, focusing on the most important, and the actual revenue goals. Remember , that if you take time to understand your WHY, it will help you to make the best decision. If you need to decide if you are going to move forward with that goal, or if you are moving it to another column for the time being. You can always revisit this at a later stage.

Let's quickly recap everything we went over so far;

- We have created the columns and arranged them in order of importance.

- We went through and identified the WHY for each of your goals, and now we are ready to step it up and continue to map out your system.

Remember that writing down your goals make them real, they also empower you in having accountability to yourself. The goal of this whole process is for you to actually achieve the goals that you set out to accomplish, so in all this, ask yourself is this a goal that I truly believe in and WHY do I believe in it?

The system itself is simple. It's a matter of you taking the system and actually working it to reach the end goal. Maybe you have already tried your hand at creating goals and structures before, so as we jump into the next chapter let's make this one work for you, and not against you.

Chapter Five

From Hot Mess To Creating Smart Goals

SMART Goals are the way to go

Congratulations! You have made it this far with me, and now we are getting down into the nitty gritty of really setting your goals. One of the sayings that rings true to me in my life came a long time ago; "The devil is in the details".

I used that all throughout my wedding planning business to really get down into the details of each and every couple's dream design. When I started my strategy business, I took that and used it for each client's project.

However, the problem was, I never used it to set my goals. It's crazy how we teach and tell our clients, kids, and friends how to achieve their goals but we don't heed that exact same advice in our own life.

Y'all, when I finally took a good, hard look at WHY I wasn't accomplishing my goals, I had to have a Margarita and say, "Dang, I have not been following my own advice." You see. it's easy to get inundated with the day to day and fall into a mundane hole, and just roll with what has been working.

But you need to ask yourself "How is that really working for me?" When I did my yearly review, I realized I was only accomplishing maybe about 50% of what I had sat out to do, and that was not ok!

So I had to change my way of goal setting and here we are - at the point where I can confidently tell you how to accomplish your goals. My final disclaimer is that this book is not magic - you are! And your goals only work when you do the work!

Next, we move on to SMART goals. SMART goals are the way to really make your goals stronger, direct, and more detail orientated . I remember when I first learned about setting SMART goals. I was like wow my goals need to be smart too!

My mind was blown as I started to jump in, and really learn what they meant by creating a SMART goal. Still, it took me quite some time to really grasp WHY I needed to focus on smart goals, and WHY it was important to actually achieve my goals.

Remember I told you I was a big dreamer, but I had to focus and be specific in defining the thing I wanted to achieve? When you set smart goals you have a better chance of reaching the finish line towards what you are trying to accomplish.

Following the steps to making your goals SMART, will help you to identify the exact goal you want to achieve and not create the overarching, lofty goals that we all start out with.

Smart Goals Stand For :

S - Specific

The goals that you set, need to be as specific as possible. When setting goals it's easy to set big lofty goals and intangible, hard-to-action goals. For example; a goal could be that you want to grow your social media following.

"Oh that's great, but it's still too big for you to actually do with nothing tangible to hold on to". So let's be specific, " I want to grow my social media following, meaning to grow my Instagram account to 10k followers, in the next three months". That's specific and tangible, this is something you can actually set to an action plan achieve.

When you leave yourself wide open, you set yourself up for failure. Goals should be something you can achieve because you have set up a plan to accomplish it.

M- Measurable

Each goal that you set needs to be measurable. If you can't measure if it's successful or not, how will you know if you've really achieved it? So how are you going to measure if this goal is successful?

Measuring your success can be a hard one for most people but you have to have measurable goals or a metric of measuring them with. If your goal is to grow your following socially, what does that look like?

A great example would be, "I have 500 followers on Instagram currently, and in the next 6 months, I want to add 500 more followers". How many followers do you need to get a month, to keep on track with that goal? Over the next couple of months you are constantly checking in to ensure you actually reach that goal. A great way of doing this, might be to set smaller milestones or check points for yourself.This pairs very well with setting that specific goal.

If your goal is a revenue goal, set smaller stage gates to check in and see if you are getting close to reaching the goal or not. Revenue goals are probably my favorite, it really shows growth in yourself and your business. They are some of the hardest ones to achieve but when you do, it's the most rewarding of the goals to achieve.

So how do we go about measuring them? We set monthly revenue goals! This month I want to make or save 500, so how many clients do I need to book or, how many service packages do I need to sell? Break that down, and know your numbers. Once you have your numbers, keep them on the side, but at a visible distance, as we will use them as we start to plan.

Check in with that goal and see if you are on track to accomplish it. Think of your goals as a part of you. Your goals are not to be perceived as your side boo - they are your main boo, and in order to accomplish them, they have to be top of mind and not second place.

Whatever you are setting goals for, we will create a system on how you plan to measure your goal to see if you are actually achieving this goal.

A- Achievable

Creating goals is already a big step, but are you creating goals that are actually achievable? See, we have touched on this several times and in order to actually fulfill the goal you set for yourself, or your business, they have to be broken down into things you can actually accomplish. So no lofty goals is the best way to say it. Large, venturesome goals are great, but more specific, more achievable goals are what we want to shoot for.

Ask yourself how achievable is my goal, when writing your smart goals, you need to think about your WHY. Is this something that you truly believe in, and can stand by? Is this something against all odds, you will be able to achieve?

This is the time you may want to do some introspection on your actual goal, to determine if this is something you have never done before. Within that research make sure you are able to accomplish every task associated in the process of attaining that specific goal.

If you have taken the time to create a goal that is specific, you should be able to achieve it , because it has a beginning and an end. Now write down all the ways you can see yourself achieving that goal.

R- Relevant

This is one of the most important questions to ask while you are in the goal setting process, WHY. WHY are you focusing on this goal? WHY is it important to you, and does it fit into your major overarching plan?

Each and every goal needs to be relevant to your broader goals. It needs to align with your WHY, your mission, your vision and your core values. If it does not, it is not relevant, and you may need to shift a bit or pivot, and make it fit into your overall plan.

Or you may want to just stick it into the "later" pile, if you are really passionate about getting it done and refocus on this goal a bit further down the line.

Relevant goals are sometimes harder to comprehend and my example is always the same, however not everyone can relate, but they understand it. If your goal as a dog walker is to have 10 thousand dollar months, you are not going to go way left, and decide to open a strip club are you?

Is that relevant in growing your existing business? No, but it's always a great idea! (LOL) The goal should be relevant to what you are hoping to accomplish. "I want to have a 10K month for my dog walking business" how many clients do I need to have, and how much do I need to charge in order to reach that benchmark?

T-Time bound

What is the deadline for this goal? Is this something that will take you a month, three months , or even a year? You need to create a deadline for your goals, one; so that you make it real, and second; so that you start to hold yourself accountable.

Giving your goals a real deadline, helps to put a fire under your butt, which in turn makes you get stuff done. So in simple form - what is the due date?

When each of your goals are broken down into actual smart goals, this will help you in creating an action plan to actually set goals that are tangible and that excites you to jump in, and get to work!

Chapter Six

Let's Plan And Celebrate

So let's get to the fun stuff, let's break it down one time and set some goals

FYI - I am so doing a happy dance, because this is truly where the magic happens. You get to see all your hard work come together, and start to see it become a reality. When I think of this part, this is where we actually get to the breakdown of setting the goals, and putting everything into actually creating a plan that will help you get closer to your goals.

This makes me think of baking a cake. Yes, friends I started my first business as a baker circa 2008, but that's for another time and another book.

When you bake a cake it first starts with the perfect recipe, the nicest ingredients, the exact measurements, the perfect temperature and lastly, the exact baking time. When you use the recipe as instructed and mix to perfection, with no over mixing, bake for 45 minutes - when it comes out of the oven, not only is it pretty, it's magic!

Your house smells amazing, and you can't wait to pipe the frosting, and eat it. That's how I want you to feel about goal setting. I want you to feel fabulous, empowered like a boss!

So if you are not excited at this point, stop and throw on your pump up song (Mine is Missy Elliot's Work-it) and do a happy dance! If you are not a dancer that's ok, do like my work family does, and hit a power pose and let's get it done!

Let's first jump into the top three principles of goal setting; they are as simple, yet equally effective such as the SMART goals you are setting.

Clarity - Each and every goal needs to be clear and very well defined. When they are clear you understand them and can break them down into actual attainable check-points.

Challenging - What's the saying: If it doesn't scare you, your goal is not big enough? This is the rule of thumb friends, we are dreaming big because H-E-L-L-O! That's what goal setting is all about. Then we are breaking it down to make it actually attainable.

Commit - I need you to commit to that goal like we committed to big hair and bad eyebrows in the 90's. If you have no clue what I am talking about please google it, it is worth the google...and giggle!

Seriously, commit to achieving this goal. Commit to achieving something bigger than yourself. Commit to finally doing the thing you have been wanting to do for so long, but haven't. Commit to your goal like I committed to writing this book.

Your goals are one of the things you have to be all in on, you can't just dip your toe in and run, you have to full-body submerge and get it done, because this is something you have been waiting for a long time.

These are the top three principles you want to remember when creating your goals. These principles will help you really dig in, and think about what you want to accomplish. This will help you start to brainstorm your goals, and help you not to get stuck in your own head.

So , now we are really ready to get to setting your goals, and first things first. Remember when you wrote down your mission statement, vision statement, core values and your WHY? Well now I want you to bring them back out. When you start to think about writing your goals we need to check in, and make sure everything aligns.

I want you to take a moment and re-read them. If you need to add anything or change anything now is the time to change it. Next, I want you to write down all of your goals for your business, life and, or finances.

Nothing is too big and nothing is too small. Take the next five to ten minutes, set a timer if you need to, and brain dump all your goals either for the next six months, nine months or the year, on individual sticky notes or on a big piece of paper.

TAKE THIS TIME TO WRITE IT ALL OUT

Now that you have all your goals written out on paper, or sticky notes, now is the time to start dropping them into your table. If these are business goals create a space for business, if they are financial create a space for financial goals, and if these are life goals create a space for life goals.

Every type of goal should have it's own bucket. Then either on the same paper, or on a different sticky note, make sure to write down your WHY, for each goal. You need to remember WHY" this goal is important, it will help you put them into perspective when you are creating your plan.

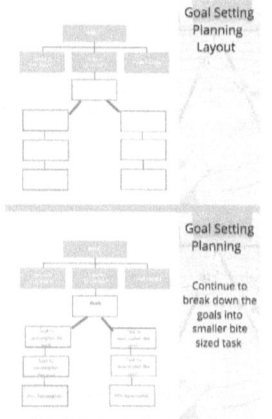

Once you have moved them into their space, reorder them in order of importance to you. Remember to check in with your mission, vision and core value statements. You can move them around the board if you have done this on sticky notes, or you can number them or color code them. Just make sure you know what's most important.

Take those goals you just wrote down, numbered, and take out the top three goals for each. If you wrote down a bunch, it's ok they may fall in with your top three, if not, you can start a separate process for them after you finish your top three.

Pulling out the top three goals is one of the biggest steps towards effective goal setting. You are taking the ones that you feel are most important in your business, personal life, or growth in your finances. Naturally, your finances of course, lead to growing your business, which in turn will help your life, so if you want to focus on all three that is fine, but make sure that is in your overarching WHY.

As we continue to break down your goals, I want you to do a once over and review, that you have really identified your top three, because once we start there are no regrets just progress.

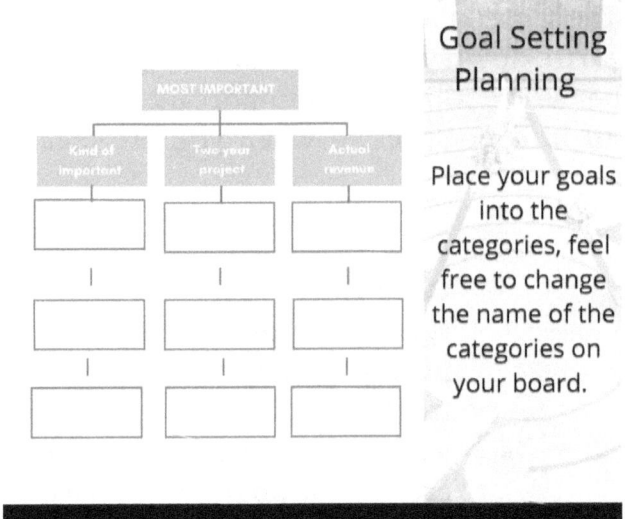

Goal Setting Planning

Place your goals into the categories, feel free to change the name of the categories on your board.

Following the identification of your top three goals in each of your categories, I want you to take each goal and give it a due date of when you want to actually get it accomplished. Think about everything that goes into actually achieving that goal, and how much time you need to make it happen and set a realistic date to it.

Here is a prime example of what not to do - "I am going to get married and I want to get married in 15 days, with 500 people on the beach, in the middle of the rainy season" Now can it happen? Yes it can. Will it be exciting? Yup, in the beginning!

But, will you wholeheartedly regret it, and not even get to enjoy the process of being engaged, enjoy being surrounded by your family and friends on your wedding day, and dancing the night away? Yup, absolutely!

Instead of it being a day of joy, you will always look back and think about how awful it was. So now you will forever think of your wedding day as a day with a cloud of should of, would of, could of!. So, let's get it right the first time.

Next let's give each of your tasks a due date and spread them out. You can use the quarter system (one goal a quarter), or you can spread them over a couple of months at a time. Just give yourself sufficient time to accomplish, reflect, and celebrate before diving head first into the next goal.

So as you are thinking of your due date, I want you to give yourself time to actually get everything done. Once you set a due date, I want you to add a week because you need to give yourself grace to get this done. You are only human, and there are going to be days that you don't want to work on that goal.

There are going to be days you just want to Netflix and chill, and friend - you should! There are going to be days where life is busy and you just don't have time and that's fine. This is not about pushing yourself to be unhappy this is about creating a schedule where you have freedom to make it happen. Remember these goals should be exciting, they should excite the hell out of you. There are going to be days where you feel like you have made no progress and you don't see the light at the end of the tunnel, and to that I say keep going. This is all about creating a space and taking your time to make it happen. You are building greatness and that doesn't happen overnight so give yourself a break.

The next step is the big one, this is where you take each of the three top goals you set, and you break down each, and every task that goes into achieving that goal. For example you need to create a website, write it down, create an email list, write it down, send an email, write it down.

The present, now, is the time for you to create a task list for yourself, as well as a guide that you can come back to in the future if you need to. Write everything down, get it out of your head and onto paper - nothing is too small when it comes to achieving your goals.

Now Let's create the plan

Well done! You've just finished writing down all the tasks associated with your major goals, now it's time to schedule everything out. Grab a calendar - either paper or digital, and I want you to first add the due dates with the respective goal to the calendar.

We are going to start from the end and work our way back to the beginning. Goal Setting is weird, I know, but when you start at the end, it will help you to lay everything out, and schedule time to get your tasks done.

Once you add your due date, you are going to now write in your task. Next, you are going to count the weeks it will take you, 'till your due date, and write your first goal on week one.

Pick one to two days a week where you are going to work on your goals. If you have time to work on something daily, schedule it daily. The idea is not to overwhelm yourself. When you get overwhelmed, you start to go back into the fight or flight mode of operating, and ain't nobody got time for that!

So let's start with one to two days a week to work on a task that will get you closer to your goals. If they are smaller tasks, batch them together. For bigger tasks, spread them out over a period of a couple of days.

Giving yourself time to accomplish each one, gives you time to breathe, time to pour into that goal a bit more, and time to truly accomplish what you've set out to achieve. Use these same steps for each one of your goals.

Give them dates, break them down into tasks, schedule them out using your deadline as an anchor and plan.

Financial goals are the same. You want to hook them to how you are going to reach those financial goals. Are you creating a product or service? Is this passive income, or how many clients you need to book?

When writing those down, you are going to want to know how many clients, or services you need to sell in order to achieve that financial goal, and then lay out how many you need to get over the weeks.

For example: "I want to make $1,500 extra this month. My package is $500 so I need to sell 1 package a week for the next 3 weeks to achieve my goal, and I have an extra week buffer to make it happen."

Now that you have hit your goal and built in a little buffer or grace period, you need to attach your financial goals (which is the what) to the "how" you are going to make that financial goal happen.

When planning your goals think about how much time you think it will take to get it done and then add a week.

These are your goals, these are milestones to your big goal. As you go through the process of setting goals and putting them on your calendar schedule in mini milestones.

When you reach them, celebrate achieving them and then keep pushing forward to reach the ultimate goal. It's as simple as that!

Creating your goals, making a plan, and tasking them out is what you have to do to make your goals a reality. See, the fact that the perception was that your goals are hard and complicated, was a total lie in the beginning, they are layered and beautiful as well.

They should absolutely scare the hell out of you, but excite you all at the same time. Your goals are the things that live on your heart. They are one of the main reasons you do the things you do.

Your goals are the reason you are here reading this book, they are not rocket science, but they are complex, and that is beautiful!

In order to achieve your goals, you have to do the work. You can read this book and re-read this book a thousand times, but if you don't take the time, and do the work you will be back at square one.every.single.time!

It's time for you to step up, stand out, and achieve the goals you have been dreaming of achieving all your life. When you achieve your goal, I want you to remember that feeling, I want you to live in that moment.

Remember how it feels, what you are feeling inside. Hold on to how excited you are, how relieved you are! How accomplished do you feel at that moment? Live in it, enjoy it, dance it out, and then do it again because you got this!

Hey Friends we made it and I am so incredibly proud of you! Normally I am doing this in person and we would celebrate with a dance party, so please do me a favor and dance it out!

Please let me know how you are doing so I can continue to support you and cheer you on. It's weird not having a face to face meeting with you, so please drop by on social media and introduce yourself. I would love to hear all about your journey.

NOW Let's Celebrate

Xoxo ~ Keneshia Renee

Acknowledgements

This book has been a long time coming and I would like to thank my family for all the support during the long writing nights. For always having wine on hand during the late night editing and pushing me when I started to second guess myself . To my dad for the love, support and believing in me.

Edward, thank you for being my best friend, my rider and support system when I need it the most. To my Startup Tucson Family Liz, Dre and Sophia, I want to say thank you, thank you for challenging me, thank you for supporting me. Thank you for making me smile during this crazy 2020, this year would have looked a lot different without you. To my homie Bjorgivin thanks friend for supporting my crazy challenge of a book in 30 days and being an awesome cohost.

Earnestine, the late night editing talks and the encouragement is so appreciated. Last but not least Wendy, girl I can not thank you enough for being my friend, my wine dealer (lol) and an amazing cheerleader through this process. Even when I wasn't feeling the negativity in my life you pushed me to get this done and I will say thank you a million times.

I could not have written this book without all of your support, encouragement and late night laughs. To my fabulous editor Sharmaine you made my work magical.

About The Author

Keneshia Renee is the founder of Blissful Creatives & KeneshiaRenee.com where she specializes in business strategy through goal setting and solid foundations. After developing successful conferences and summits, and speaking at various events and conferences, she knew she wanted to do even more. She found a love for tech, mentoring and educating small businesses, early-stage startups with a focus on women in business.

She has been working as a mentor for startup based companies, working with women to define and grow their business and prepare to pitch to investors. She also teaches and mentors through numerous non-profits.

Originally from Los Angeles California, she is excited

to embrace Tucson's way of life and help grow business here. Having started in the food, tech and wedding sec